Zoom in on the BALD EAGLE

ZOOM in on American Symbols

Heather Moore Niver

Enslow Publishing
101 W. 23rd Street
Suite 240
New York, NY 10011
USA
enslow.com

WORDS TO KNOW

document A piece of paper giving information or proof of something.

motto A brief phrase that sums up a person's or group's beliefs.

official Recognized by the government or other authority.

represent To stand for.

seal A stamp that is usually decorative.

symbol An image or shape that stands for another thing.

talon A bird's claw.

wingspan The distance from the tip of one wing to the other.

CONTENTS

Eagles can fly up to 30 miles (48 kilometers) an hour. When they dive they can reach 100 miles (161 km) an hour.

Bald Eagle Basics

Every state in America has an official flower, motto, and bird. But did you know that the United States of America has a national bird, too? The bald eagle can be seen on all kinds of items used all over the country. For example, the eagle is on coins, paper bills, and even the official seal of the president. Keep reading to find out how this big bird became a national symbol.

The Bald Eagle Isn't Bald

The bald eagle has a bright white head of feathers. It isn't bald at all! The rest of its body is covered with brown feathers, which just makes its head look like the bird is bald. Most eagles measure between 34 and 43 inches (86 to 109 centimeters) long. Their wingspan can be anywhere from 6 to 8 feet

All-American Bird

President John F. Kennedy wrote, "The founding fathers made an appropriate choice when they selected the bald eagle as the emblem of the nation. The fierce beauty and proud independence of this great bird aptly symbolizes the strength and freedom of America."

The white feathers on a bald eagle's head make it look bald.

(1.8 to 2.4 meters) across. An average eagle weighs around 6.5 to 14 pounds (3 to 6.5 kilograms). That's one big bird!

Selecting a Symbol

On July 4, 1776, a group of Americans signed the Declaration of Independence. This document made America's independence from Great Britain official. One step they took was to decide on some national symbols. Many countries around the world have a special animal to represent their country. England's symbol is a lion, and India's is a peacock. Thomas Jefferson, John Adams, and Benjamin Franklin had

The official design for the American seal was approved on June 20, 1782.

the job of choosing a design for an official national seal.

Disagreements

Unfortunately, while they agreed about independence, the three men had a hard time agreeing on what their symbol should be. Finally, Jefferson, Adams, and Franklin decided on a design that did not include an animal at all! Instead, it was based on a woman, "Liberty," who held a shield. The shield represented all the states.

Lady Liberty

The Statue of Liberty, sometimes called "Lady Liberty," is a statue that stands 151 feet (46 m) tall. It is located just off the coast of New York City. It was a gift from France in 1886.

But Congress did not agree with the design. They talked with an artist named William Barton. Barton created a design that featured the golden eagle. They liked it but decided on the American bald eagle instead of the golden eagle. This is because the bald eagle lives only in America and not in Europe.

Facts and Fiction

There are many stories about the choice of the eagle as the official national bird for the United States of America. One of the most popular stories is that Benjamin Franklin wanted a different bird than the bald eagle.

Turkey Tales

One of the most popular stories about the eagle and its place as the US national bird involves Benjamin Franklin. It says

Benjamin Franklin was not a fan of the bald eagle as the national symbol, but he did not really suggest it should be a turkey instead.

The Turkey Seal?

Stories that Benjamin Franklin really wanted the turkey to replace the eagle were thought to be real after a 1962 cover of *New Yorker* magazine. Artist Anatole Kovarsky showed what the seal would look like by creating it with a turkey.

that Franklin was against the eagle and that he wanted the turkey instead! This is only partly true. Franklin did provide a different design for an official seal, but it didn't include a bird at all. It is true that he was not crazy about choosing the eagle. He wrote a letter to his daughter pointing out that the eagle hunts by stealing meals that other animals have already killed. Franklin did not think

these were actions that should represent America. In the letter he wonders if the turkey would have been a better choice.

The President of the United States has a special seal, which features the bald eagle symbol.

Changes

The eagle is a part of many national seals and designs. The Presidential Seal shows the bird holding an olive branch in one talon and thirteen arrows in the other. (The olive branch is a symbol of peace, and the arrows stand for war, which is sometimes needed to protect the country.) But the Presidential Seal has not always looked exactly the same. The reason for its change is another interesting story in American history.

You can see the old design of the Presidential Seal on this desk where President Barack Obama sits working in the White House.

A Symbol of Peace

When the Presidential Seal was first designed, the eagle's beak faced the right, toward the arrows it held in its talons. The seal looked like this from 1916 to 1945. But President Harry S. Truman had it changed. He wanted the eagle to face the olive branches on the left. This change showed the country's dedication to peace. A desk in

Changing Times

President Truman showed British leader Winston Churchill his new design. Churchill is said to have joked that the eagle's head should be able to rotate because the country was in and out of war!

President Harry S. Truman had the eagle on the seal change direction. He thought it should face the more peaceful olive branches.

the White House still shows the first design of the seal with the eagle facing the arrows.

It is true that Truman made the change after a war. Later, however, rumors started that the seal was changed depending on whether or not the country was at war or at peace. This is not true. Stories that have been told in books and on television make the story seem true! The seal has actually stayed the same since Truman's time.

The US national seal is found on monuments like the World War II Memorial in Washington, DC.

ACTIVITY
NATIONAL SYMBOLS AROUND THE WORLD

Countries all around the world have special national symbols to represent their country. Use this research activity to find out more about the national birds and other national symbols around the world.

1. Using a globe, map, or atlas, pick four countries from different areas of the world. Draw a picture of each country or print out a picture from the Internet.

2. Using the Internet, atlas, or books in the library, look up information about each country. If you need help, ask a parent, teacher, or librarian to direct you to books or websites that will help you find this information.

3. Do these countries have national symbols? Draw a picture of each symbol or print each one out from the Internet.

4. How do these countries use their symbol? For example, do they show it on flags or seals? How do they use it differently than the United States does? Why did they choose this symbol?

5. Has their symbol or seal ever changed in any way? Write down any changes or print out different pictures of the symbol or seal.

6. If any of the countries do not have a special symbol, what would you choose as their national bird? Print out a picture or draw it yourself and explain why you chose this bird.

7. Combine your information for each country's official or chosen symbol.

LEARN MORE

Books

Eldridge, Alison. *The Bald Eagle*. New York, NY: Enslow Elementary, 2012.

Marcovitz, Hal. *Bald Eagle: The Story of Our National Bird*. Philadelphia, PA: Mason Crest, 2015.

Nelson, Maria. *The Bald Eagle*. New York, NY: Gareth Stevens, 2015.

Websites

Ben's Guide to the US Government
bensguide.gpo.gov/j-bald-eagle
Get facts and history about the bald eagle.

A to Z Kids Stuff
atozkidsstuff.com/baldeagle.html
Learn about American symbols, including the bald eagle!

INDEX

Published in 2017 by Enslow Publishing, LLC.
101 W. 23rd Street, Suite 240, New York, NY 10011

Cataloging-in-Publication Data
Names: Niver, Heather Moore.
Title: Zoom in on the bald eagle / Heather Moore Niver.
Description: New York : Enslow Publishing, 2017 | Series: Zoom in on American symbols | Includes bibliographical references and index.
Identifiers: ISBN 9780766084421 (pbk.) | ISBN 9780766084445 (library bound) | ISBN 9780766084438 (6 pack)
Subjects: LCSH: Bald eagle—United States—Juvenile literature. | Emblems, National—United States—Juvenile literature. | Animals—Symbolic aspects—Juvenile literature. | Signs and symbols—United States—Juvenile literature. | United States—Seal—Juvenile literature.

Classification: LCC CD5610.N58 2017 | DDC 929.9—dc23

Printed in China

Photos Credits: Cover, p. 1 (inset) Wolfgang Kaehler/LightRocket/Getty Images; cover, p. 1 (background flag) Stillfx/Shutterstock.com; p. 4 Steve Jamsa/Shutterstock.com; p. 7 Harold Stiver/Shutterstock.com; p. 9 Library of Congress Prints and Photographs Division; p. 10 dwphotos/Shutterstock.com; p. 13 GraphicaArtis/Archive Photos/Getty Images; p. 15 Marshall/Hulton Archive/Getty Images; p. 17 Official White House Photo by Pete Souza; p. 19 FPG/Archive Photos/Getty Images; p. 21 Tim Mainiero/Shutterstock.com; interior pages graphic elements amtitus/DigitalVision Vectors/Getty Images (flag page borders), funnybank/DigitalVision Vectors/Getty Images (flag in circle), ly86/DigitalVision Vectors/Getty Images (eagle).